SCHOLASTIC

writing gu[ide]

With interactive resources on CD-ROM

Reports

for ages
5-7

Huw Thomas

Credits

Author
Huw Thomas

Development Editors
Simret Brar and
Rachel Mackinnon

Editor
Jenny Regan

Assistant Editor
Suzanne Adams

Series Designer
Anna Oliwa

Designer
Paul Stockmans

Book Layout
Quadrum Solutions Ltd

Cover Illustration
Mark Oliver

Illustrations
Garry Davies

CD-ROM Development
CD-ROM developed in
association with Infuze Ltd

Mixed Sources
Product group from well-managed
forests and other controlled sources
www.fsc.org Cert no. TT-COC-002769
© 1996 Forest Stewardship Council
FSC

Text © 2002, 2010 Huw Thomas
© 2010 Scholastic Ltd

Designed using Adobe InDesign

Published by Scholastic Ltd,
Book End,
Range Road,
Witney,
Oxfordshire
OX29 0YD

www.scholastic.co.uk

Printed by Bell & Bain

1 2 3 4 5 6 7 8 9   0 1 2 3 4 5 6 7 8 9

British Library Cataloguing-in-Publication Data
A catalogue record for this book is available from the British Library.

ISBN 978-1407-11266-4

CD-ROM Minimum specifications:		
Windows 2000/XP/Vista	Mac OSX 10.4	
Processor: 1 GHz	RAM: 512 MB	Graphics card: 32bit
Audio card: Yes	CD-ROM drive speed: 8x	Hard disk space: 200MB
Screen resolution: 800x600		

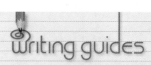

Contents

Introduction: Reports

The *Writing Guides* series aims to inspire and motivate children as writers by using creative approaches. Each *Writing Guide* contains activities and photocopiable resources designed to develop children's understanding of a particular genre (for example, fairy stories). The activities are in line with the requirements of the National Curriculum and the recommendations in the *Primary Framework for Literacy*. The teacher resource books are accompanied by a CD-ROM containing a range of interactive activities and resources.

What's in the book?

The *Writing Guides* series provides a structured approach to developing children's writing. Each book is divided into four sections.

Section 1: **Using good examples**
Three text extracts are provided to explore the typical features of the genre.

Section 2: **Developing writing**
There are ten short, focussed writing tasks in this section. These are designed to develop children's ability to use the key features of the genre in their own writing. The teacher's notes explain the objective of each activity and provide guidance on delivery, including how to use the photocopiable pages and the materials on the CD-ROM.

Section 3: **Writing**
The three writing projects in this section require the children to produce an extended piece of writing using the key features of the genre.

Section 4: **Review**
This section consists of a 'Self review', 'Peer review' and 'Teacher review'. These can be used to evaluate how effectively the children have met the writing criteria for the genre.

What's on the CD-ROM?

The accompanying CD-ROM contains a range of motivating activities and resources. The activities can be used for independent work or can be used on an interactive whiteboard to enhance group teaching.
Each CD-ROM contains:

- three text extracts that illustrate the typical features of the genre
- interactive versions of selected photocopiable pages
- four photographs and an audio file to create imaginative contexts for writing
- a selection of writing templates and images which can be used to produce extended pieces of writing.

The interactive activities on the CD-ROM promote active learning and support a range of teaching approaches and learning styles. For example, drag and drop and sequencing activities will support kinaesthic learners.

Talk for writing

Each *Writing Guide* uses the principles of 'Talk for writing' to support children's writing development by providing opportunities for them to rehearse ideas orally in preparation for writing. 'Talk for writing' is promoted using a variety of teaching strategies including discussions, questioning and drama activities (such as, developing imaginative dialogue – see *Fantasy Stories for Ages 9–11*).

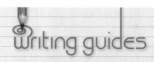

How to use the CD-ROM

Start screen: click on the 'Start' button to go to the main menu.

This section contains brief instructions on how to use the CD-ROM. For more detailed guidance, go to 'How to use the CD-ROM' on the start screen or click on the 'Help' button located in the top right-hand corner of the screen.

Installing the CD-ROM

Follow the instructions on the disk to install the CD-ROM onto your computer. Once the CD-ROM is installed, navigate to the program location and double click on the program icon to open it.

Main menu screen

Main menu

The main menu provides links to all of the writing activities and resources on the CD-ROM. Clicking on a button from the main menu will take you to a sub-menu that lists all of the activities and resources in that section. From here you have the option to 'Launch' the interactive activities, which may contain more than one screen, or print out the activities for pupils to complete by hand.

If you wish to return to a previous menu, click the 'Menu' button in the top right-hand corner of the screen; this acts as a 'back' button.

Screen tools

A range of simple writing tools that can be used in all of the writing activities are contained in the toolbar at the bottom of the screen.

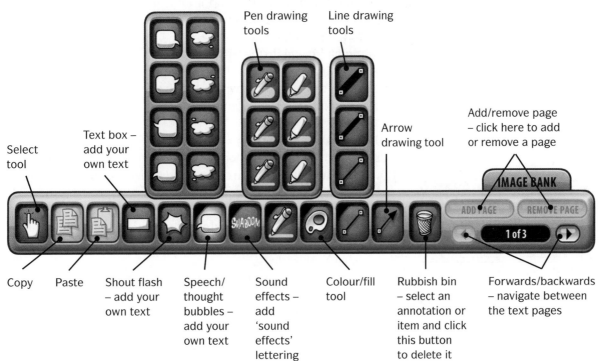

Pen drawing tools

Line drawing tools

Add/remove page – click here to add or remove a page

Arrow drawing tool

Text box – add your own text

Select tool

Copy   Paste   Shout flash – add your own text   Speech/ thought bubbles – add your own text   Sound effects – add 'sound effects' lettering   Colour/fill tool   Rubbish bin – select an annotation or item and click this button to delete it   Forwards/backwards – navigate between the text pages

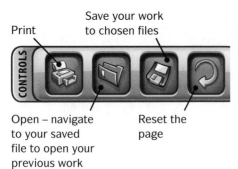

Print

Save your work to chosen files

Open – navigate to your saved file to open your previous work

Reset the page

Printing and saving work

All of the resources on the CD-ROM are printable. You can also save and retrieve any annotations made on the writing activities. Click on the 'Controls' tab on the right-hand side of the screen to access the 'Print', 'Open', 'Save' and 'Reset screen' buttons.

View all thumbnails by clicking on the arrows

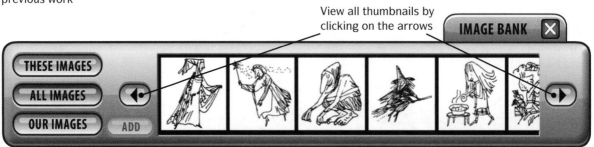

Image bank – click and drag an image to add it to an activity

Image bank

Each CD-ROM has an 'Image bank' containing images appropriate to the genre being taught. Click on the tab at the bottom right of the screen to open the 'Image bank'. On the left-hand side there are three large buttons.

- The 'These images' button will display only the images associated with the specific activity currently open.
- The 'All images' button will display all the photographs and illustrations available on the CD-ROM.
- The 'Our images' button will contain any images you or the children have added to the CD-ROM.

Press the left or right arrows to scroll through the images available. Select an image and drag and drop it into the desired location on the screen. If necessary, resize the image using the arrow icon that appears at the bottom right of the image.

You can upload images to the 'Image bank', including digital photographs or images drawn and scanned into the computer. Click on 'Our images' and then 'Add' to navigate to where the image is stored. A thumbnail picture will be added to the gallery.

Writing your own story

Each CD-ROM contains a selection of blank writing templates. The fiction genre templates will be categorised under the button 'My story' and the non-fiction templates will be categorised under 'My recount' or 'My writing'. The writing templates encourage the children to produce an extended piece of genre writing. They can also add images, speech bubbles and use other tools to enhance their work.

The fiction titles also include a cover template for the children to use. They can customise their cover by adding their own title, blurb and images.

Section 1
Using good examples

Reports

Report texts give a picture of a subject in words. They are the sort of text you find if you look up an animal in an encyclopedia or a location in a guide book – less narrative, with more statements. To do this, they often use a structure where general statements act as main points on a subject, and are then broken down into details. As a non-chronological picture of a subject, reports tend to be in the present tense and tend to be impersonal. They will veer between general and specific subjects, and provide a great means for children to express some of the facts they uncover about everything from science to football teams and, as such, are some of the most exciting writing texts on which children can embark.

Links to the Primary Framework

Report writing features in the Key Stage 1 requirements of the Literacy Framework. It provides a vital genre for promoting composition – giving children a clear subject matter around which to devise statements. The clear sentence structure also develops a good basis for factual writing.

Using good examples

This section presents children with a set of good examples of report writing from typical texts they could readily encounter. Extract 1 is about a general subject, snails being quite common animals. Extract 2 focuses on a specific place, in this case a school. Extract 3 is an example of travel writing, a common and popular form of report text that children can readily adapt to their own favourite places. In each of the extracts, a subject is introduced and the text subdivides the subject matter into basic paragraphs – this is how many report texts work. They open with general statements and then qualify these statements with more detail. They are like photographs in writing.

Subject matter

One thing that is vital in good report writing is that there is some enthusiasm or connection to the subject matter. As you read the extracts with the children, it is important to keep in mind the goal that they should write their own texts about their own subjects. When encouraging young report writers, content is everything – which is why, in the sections that follow, you will find activities adaptable to children's own enthusiasms.

Report features

Structure
- Presents a picture in words.
- Organises information.
- Moves from general to specific statements.
- Gives details.

Language
- States how something is or what it is like; technical vocabulary.
- Present-tense sentences.

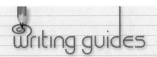

Extract 1: Snails

This extract takes a subject familiar to the children and uses it as the basis to show how one child structures a good example of report writing.

- Open Extract 1 from the CD-ROM and read through the text. Ask the children to read the sentences with you, one paragraph at a time. At the end of each paragraph, ask: *What did that tell us?* Use the tools to annotate the extract with answers given by the children.

- Once they have finished reading the extract, ask the children to look at each paragraph and suggest what it is about snails that that paragraph tackles. Highlight how each paragraph has a different focus.

- Hand out copies of photocopiable page 10 'Extract 1: Snails'. Ask the children to pick out the information in the text by circling one word or phrase that is a fact about snails. You could create a list of facts.

- Open '"Snails" notes' from the CD-ROM and explain how Nadia's writing from the extract has been translated into her planning notes. Ask the children to find the sentences in the extract that relate to the notes and to type in the answers on screen.

- Hand out copies of photocopiable page 14 '"Snails" notes' and ask the children to compare Nadia's notes to the extract, circling the notes that appear in the main text.

Extract 2: Springwood

Children read a formal text, analyse it and compare it with a less formal one. They create sentences about their own school.

- Hand out photocopiable page 11 'Extract 2: Springwood' and read the text together. Ask the children to think about what sort of person might have written it and who it is for.

- Contrast the text with Nadia's more informal text in Extract 1. What makes this one feel more formal? Can they see a difference between the first and second paragraphs?

- Open Extract 2 from the CD-ROM and use the tools to highlight the way the extract gives a background to the subject, some details about the current numbers in the school and one interesting and unique fact about the place – the language diversity. The second paragraph is less factual and centres more on what the school is like.

- Ask the children to think of similar sentences they could write about their own school. Their examples could be classed as 'Paragraph A sentences (facts)' or 'Paragraph B sentences (opinions)'. Once completed, compare them with a copy of the school's prospectus.

- Hand out photocopiable page 15 'Use the text' or use the version on the CD-ROM. Ask the children to answer the questions, using information from the extract. Encourage them to highlight the source of their answers on the extract.

Extract 3: Who is Big Ben?

This extract works best if the children do some thinking beforehand, working on the whole idea of inquiry and report as an answer.

What's on the CD-ROM

Media resources
- Use the 'Big Ben' image as a stimulus for discussion.

Who is Big Ben?
- Report text in the style of travel writing information to read, discuss and edit.

Big Ben questions
- Roll your mouse over questions to find where the answers appear in the extract.

- Ask the children to find out about Big Ben – listening out for it on the radio, seeing it on the television and so on. Encourage them to devise some questions about Big Ben.

- Open the image 'Big Ben' from the CD-ROM. Collate the children's questions and write them on the whiteboard. Hand out photocopiable pages 12 and 13 'Extract 3: Who is Big Ben?' and read through the extract together. Ask the children to look at the questions they have asked, seeing which ones have been answered by the text.

- Open Extract 3 from the CD-ROM. Explain that the extract can be edited on screen. Delete some of the sentences and ask the children to re-enter the same information, but in their own words. Encourage them to redraft a whole section.

- Open 'Big Ben questions' from the CD-ROM and see whether the suggestions match their own question ideas. Can the children find the answers to the questions in the extract? Hand out photocopiable page 16 'Big Ben questions' (enlarged if necessary) and ask the children to work as a group to answer the questions. When they have done this, roll your mouse over the question marks on the on-screen activity to see where the information can be found in the original report.

Poster: Reports

The poster sums up some of the main features of report texts that children will have encountered in their reading. It gives the four main features which children need to work at in their own texts.

What's on the CD-ROM

Reports
- Roll your mouse over each section of the poster to reveal further information, which will enable you to link good examples to the guidance that underpins Section 2 of this book.

- The poster illustrates the main genre features of reports: introduction and organisation of a subject, with details, in the present tense. As they look through the features on the poster, ask the children if they know what each one means and, as you build on this understanding, ask them to locate examples in Extracts 1, 2 and 3.

- As an introduction to the poster, use photocopiable page 17 'Report jumble' as a way of revisiting two of the texts and observing the job they do.

- Open the 'Reports' poster from the CD-ROM and roll your mouse over each section to reveal more information which you can use to illustrate the points. Ask the children to start thinking about their own subject matter and how they could write in a way that covers these guidelines.

- As the children work on report writing, keep referring back to the poster. Hand out photocopiable page 18 'Reports' that can be annotated, torn up, used to make notes on and so on. Make the poster a central feature of this writing project.

Extract 1: Snails

Snails are small animals. They live in the garden. Snails usually live in dark places, like under stones or in old flower pots.

A snail has a hard shell that is usually brown and white, and a soft body. The soft body is called a foot. If a snail moves across glass and you look underneath it, you can see little lines moving down the foot. Snails move slowly. The snail's shell can grow. Every time it grows it adds another stripe to its pattern.

At the end of the foot there are two pairs of tentacles. A snail uses a lower pair for touching and smelling. The upper tentacles have got two eyes at the end. They also have a mouth.

A snail likes to eat fresh leaves and tomatoes. Its droppings are usually the same colour as its food. If it eats green food, its droppings are green. If it eats tomatoes, its droppings are red.

It can be relaxing to watch a snail.

by Nadia Rafia

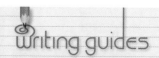

Extract 2: Springwood

The School

Springwood is one of Sheffield's historic schools, built by the Sheffield School Board in 1875. Currently the school has pupils aged between 3 and 11 years. It has a 26-place Nursery for children under school age. There are 210 children at the school. The school is lively and interesting – with the children speaking 18 different languages.

The school provides good quality teaching in a calm, working environment. The school aims to maintain good relationships with the local community, respecting one another and working together.

> "Pupils love coming to school and enjoy their learning."
> Springwood OFSTED Inspection Report

Illustrations © 2002, Garry Davies.

Extract 3: Who is Big Ben?

Many people recognise the sight of the clock tower on the Houses of Parliament, known as Big Ben. In fact, Big Ben isn't the name of the tower, or even the clock.

The tower is called the Clock Tower. It is a 96 metre tower at one end of the Houses of Parliament. There is a light at the top of the tower that is lit whenever the MPs, the people who make laws for the land, are working at night.

At the bottom of the tower there are the rooms where the Sergeant at Arms – a policeman for Parliament – can keep any naughty MPs in detention (this last happened in 1880).

The clock is huge – four dials, each seven metres across. The Roman numerals on the clock are 60cm long and each minute space is 30cm. The clock is an old type of clock that uses weights to make it 'tick tock' along. To make the weights really accurate, they use old pennies. Each penny

Illustrations © 2010, Garry Davies.

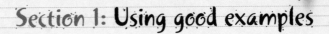

added to the weights makes the clock go about a second a week faster! To wash the clock, cleaners need to dangle by ropes – something that only gets done every five years.

So who is 'Ben'? Ben is the big bell inside that makes the chime you sometimes hear on news programmes, striking the hours. The bell weighs 16,300kg! The long tune the clock plays every hour comes from a piece written by the composer, Handel, to which the words are, 'Lord, through this hour, be thou our guide'. You could try singing along!

'Big Ben' may have been named after the man who looked after the building of Parliament, Sir Benjamin Hall, or a famous prize fighter, Benjamin Caunt.

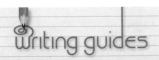

Section 1: Using good examples

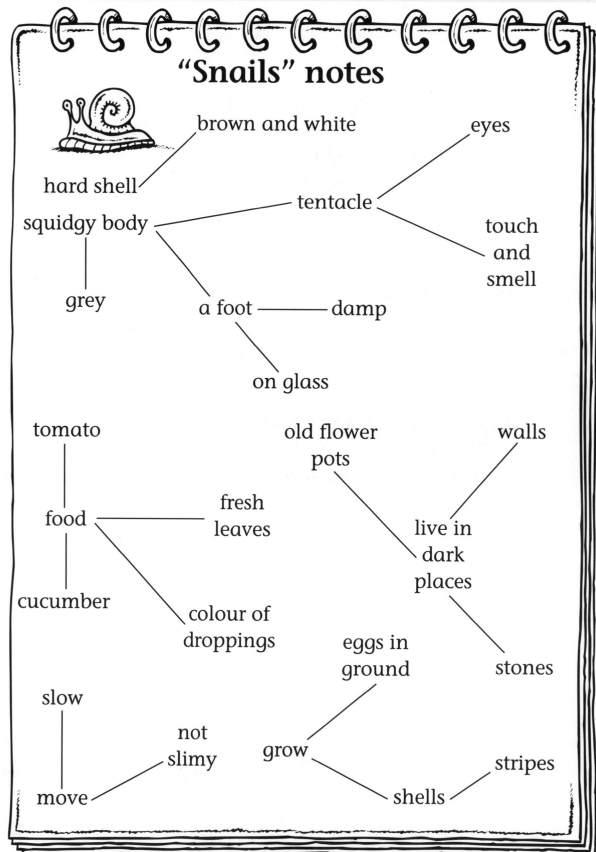

"Snails" notes

brown and white   eyes

hard shell

squidgy body   tentacle   touch and smell

grey   a foot ——— damp

on glass

tomato   old flower pots   walls

food   fresh leaves   live in dark places

cucumber

colour of droppings   eggs in ground   stones

slow

not slimy   grow   stripes

move   shells

Illustrations © 2002, Garry Davies.

● Here are Nadia's notes for her snail report. Circle things in her notes that you can find in her writing.

Use the text

● Use the text to answer these questions about Springwood School.

Where is Springwood?

How old are the pupils?

When was it built?

How many places are there in the Nursery?

How many children are there in the school?

What do the children think of the school?

How many languages are there in the school?

Illustrations © 2002, Garry Davies.

Big Ben questions

● Cut out these questions and share them among your group. Use the text to become experts in Big Ben and answer the questions.

Who or what is 'Big Ben'?	Where is it?
How tall is the tower?	What is on top?
How big is the clock?	How does the clock work?
How do they clean the clock?	What is the tune it chimes?
What else is inside the tower?	Why is it called 'Ben' ?

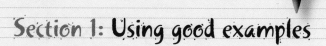

Report jumble

● Here are some facts from the two report texts. They are split up and mixed up. Cut them out and put them back together to complete the facts.

✂

The school is	Springwood is
two pairs of tentacles.	Snails are
The soft body is	small animals.
lively and interesting.	pupils aged between 3 and 11 years.
Currently the school has	a hard shell.
It has	one of Sheffield's historic schools.
At the end of the foot there are	a 26-place Nursery.
A snail has	called a foot.

Reports

**Introduce
a subject**  Snails are small animals...

**Give some
details**  It has a 26-place Nursery...

...children speaking 18 different languages.

**Use present
tense**  The soft body is called a foot...

Snails move slowly...

**Organise
information** At the end of the foot there are two pairs of tentacles...

The upper tentacles have...

Illustrations © 2002, Garry Davies.

Section 2
Developing writing

Developing report writing

Report texts present information about a subject, in a form that can be likened to a photograph in words. Whereas recounts tell events over time and explanations describe a process as it develops, report texts take a subject and present it in a timeless form.

Subject matter is a significant feature of report writing. Children need direct stimulus that engages them with the subject of their writing – if they are writing about pets, they need to see some.

Gathering and organising information

Referring back to 'Extract 3: Who is Big Ben?' (photocopiable pages 12 and 13), you will see an example of the way in which a report text takes a subject and explores it. Report texts gather a range of information and then organise it into sections that enable the reader to digest the facts. To do this, the writer needs to identify the key features of a subject and use these as the guiding principle in organising the paragraphs that follow – so rather than mix facts about the size of the clock with details of what's inside, each feature has its own section.

Detail

Report texts thrive on facts and details. They are designed to inform the reader, so rather than just telling us about the Big Ben we have seen on the television, they take us inside and tell us about the pennies used as weights. To do this, they need to move from the general to the specific, in a hierarchical arrangement. Each paragraph may flag up a different aspect of the subject, and the sentences that follow take their place under that label.

Language features

Report texts are snapshots and, as such, tend to use the timeless present tense. They do not say how the life cycle of a snail moves from one stage to another, they rather present a picture of what a snail is and what its features are. They also benefit from adjectives that make the subject matter more vivid and may contain technical or subject-specific vocabulary.

Activity breakdown

Planning
- Things to say (page 20)
- Pick it apart (page 20)
- Superheroic reporting (page 21)

Layout
- Tree splits (page 21)
- About me (page 22)
- About us (page 23)
- Same but more (page 24)

Language
- Is, are, has, have (page 22)
- Subject cards (page 23)
- Adjectives game (page 24)

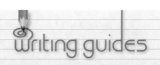

Activity 1: Things to say

Objectives

To independently choose what to write about, plan and follow it through. (Year 1 Strand 9)
To write chronological and non-chronological texts using simple structures. (Year 1 Strand 10)

What to do

Choosing from a range of objects you bring into school, the children start to report on a subject.

- Display a range of objects and ask a child to select one of them. Invite the class to say everything they can about the object, for example, what it looks like, what it is made from and so on.

- Give a brief description of the physical nature of the object to the class and make some simple notes on a flipchart. Focus on another object and gather a range of comments about it, noting these on the chart. Repeat the process with several other objects.

- When you have finished, look at the list of comments you have collected and, using different-coloured marker pens, circle similar comments. For example, if the colour of the object has elicited comments, circle these in one colour. If different moving parts have been commented on, circle those in another.

- Cut out the headings on an enlarged copy of photocopiable page 25 'Object features' and, one by one, group the features you have listed under these headings. Tear up the flipchart and ask the children to stand with the feature in the relevant place.

- Hand out photocopiable page 25 'Object features' and ask the children to list the features of other objects under each heading.

Activity 2: Pick it apart

Objectives

To independently choose what to write about, plan and follow it through. (Year 1 Strand 9)
To write chronological and non-chronological texts using simple structures. (Year 1 Strand 10)

What to do

The children build an organised set of notes on a subject of their choice.

- Ask each child to think of a subject about which they could write. They could think of a place, such as their bedroom, an animal or a favourite object, the weirder the better as they will find more to write about! Ask them to write down the title of their subject in the middle box on photocopiable page 26 'Pick it apart'.

- Encourage the children to think of ten different things they could say about their subject. For example, if it is their bedroom: 'it has two windows', 'a matching rug and blind', 'a teddy on my bed'. If it is an animal: 'it has a beak', 'pointed ears', 'a yellow head' and so on.

- Record the ideas in note form, filling in each of the ten boxes on the photocopiable sheet. Once the children have completed as many as they can, they should write their score in the space provided.

- As a further activity, the children could use the notes they have made on the photocopiable sheet to write sentences about their subject. Ask them to think carefully about which fact to put first.

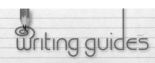

Activity 3: Superheroic reporting

Objectives

To independently choose what to write about, plan and follow it through. (Year 1 Strand 9)
To make adventurous word and language choices appropriate to the style and purpose of the text. (Year 2 Strand 9)

What to do

This activity involves constructing a report paragraph using a set of characters from a current television programme/film or craze that is generating a lot of enthusiasm.

● In a shared session, ask the children to think of a creature who has a starring role or special characteristics that would make it interesting as the subject of a report. Invite them to list different things about the character, for example, 'it has a spiral on its belly' and so on.

● Using photocopiable page 27 'Superheroic reporting', ask the children to draw their character in the centre, then use the spaces around it to pick apart some of its features, prompted by the notes around the edge. Make sure they use the sort of adventurous and exciting language such characters conjure up for them.

● Once four or five features have been listed, ask the children how they would turn the facts into sentences. Which fact would they put first? Work through each feature, turning it into a report sentence.

● When the children have completed a paragraph on one character, they can try it with another. These paragraphs will then form a simple report text, providing snapshot views of a current craze.

Activity 4: Tree splits

Objective

To group written sentences together in chunks of meaning or subject. (Year 1 Strand 10)

What's on the CD-ROM

Tree splits
● Write notes to start and continue the process of splitting subject matter, enabling children to see the organisation of their material.

What to do

This activity develops the movement from general to specific statements about a subject. In learning to do this, children both develop detail and the organising of the structure of writing.

● Open 'Tree splits' from the CD-ROM. Ask the children to begin with a subject (such as a place or a toy) and type it in the left-hand box.

● Encourage them to think of three distinct features of the subject. If, for example, they are writing about the park, they may write 'The park' on the left and, in the spaces leading from it, record 'swings', 'climbing frame' and 'lots of trees'.

● Having done this, choose which of the three features are to be further developed. Add text boxes from the toolbar around the feature to develop sub-categories containing specific statements. Repeat for the other two features by adding more boxes.

● Finally, ask the children to help you group together all of the general and specific notes made on each feature of the subject and write them in the final three text boxes on screen.

● Hand out photocopiable page 28 'Tree splits' and encourage the children to think of their own subject to write about. Remind them to develop sub-categories for each of the three distinct features, by adding notes around the three middle boxes.

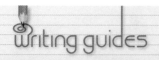

Activity 5: About me

What to do

The best subject matter is the things that children know – so why not start with themselves as a means of getting some good material.

- Open 'About me' from the CD-ROM and explain to the children that this will present them with a range of questions, building up material for a report about themselves.

- Ask the children to complete the first part of the on-screen activity, by answering the questions about themselves.

- When they have answered the questions, print out their responses and invite the children to swap their information with a partner. Using each other's answers and facts about themselves, encourage the children to fill in the spaces to create an example of a simple report text about each other in the second part of the activity.

- Hand out photocopiable page 29 'About me'. The children can complete the boxes and cut them out, sorting them into the order they would like them to appear in a report text about themselves.

- Ask the children to write a simple report about themselves, referring to the order in which they have placed the cards.

Activity 6: Is, are, has, have

What to do

This activity can be done as a guided or individual task.

- Explain to the children that report writing talks about how things 'are' and so uses the present tense.

- Open 'Is, are, has, have' from the CD-ROM and ask the children to look at the sentence starters, middles and endings. Explain that they need to drag and drop the middles and endings into the spaces to create sentences that make sense, without having any sections left over.

- Experiment with different combinations to explore the way in which some work and some do not. An important part of this task is the children getting their attempts wrong and realising that the sentences created do not sound right. Saying them aloud is a vital step in distinguishing whether sentences work or not.

- At some point, ask the children to discuss the way sentence middles work in some places but not in others. For example: If we start with 'Joe' there are two links that could work and two that couldn't. Regardless of the sentence opening, 'is' can link to some things but not to others.

- Hand out photocopiable page 30 'Is, are, has, have'. Encourage the children to complete the photocopiable sheet to reinforce the idea of grammatical consistency.

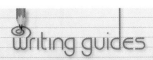

Activity 7: Subject cards

Objective

To convey information and ideas in simple non-narrative forms. (Year 1 Strand 9)

What's on the CD-ROM

Subject cards

- Roll your mouse over a subject to reveal questions to ask about it, as a means of demonstrating the way to convey information through report texts.

What to do

This activity focuses on making notes to write a report about a subject.

- Open 'Subject cards' from the CD-ROM and ask the children to roll the mouse over the subjects on each screen. Read out the questions as they appear.

- Choose one of the subjects to discuss and, as a class, answer the roll-over questions. Can the children think of any other questions they can ask that would reveal more information about that subject?

- Ask the children to cut out the subject cards from photocopiable page 31 'Subject cards'. Place the cards face down on the table. Explain that children should select a card, turn it face upwards and make some notes about that subject on a piece of paper. These may be short phrases or words, as in photocopiable page 14 '"Snails" notes', but they should have the makings of a report text. Once they have done this, explain that they need to imagine they are going to use their notes to write a report about the subject, remembering to use the present tense. Ask the children to write a few of the sentences that could feature in such a text.

- Keep referring back to 'Subject cards' on the CD-ROM to show the sorts of question that can unpick a subject.

Activity 8: About us

Objective

To draw on knowledge and experience of texts in deciding and planning what and how to write. (Year 2 Strand 9)

What to do

This activity provides an opportunity for the children to turn their writing into a report on the class.

- Divide the class into groups of four to six. Ask each group to read all the reports for the children in their group, which were completed in Activity 5.

- As they do this, encourage them to make notes on photocopiable page 32 'About us' for the areas selected, to find out certain things about the group.

- Explain that you would like the children to write a report sentence or paragraph about their group, focusing on one or two facts that they have found out. This could be something as simple as the different eye colours in the group, for example, 'Two of the group have blue eyes and four have brown eyes', or it could be a statement that presents a brief summary, such as 'Everyone in the group is the same age, but we all have different favourite foods'.

- Point out that it may be interesting to note the ways in which they are similar and different, comparing their original writing.

Activity 9: Same but more

Objective

To make adventurous word and language choices appropriate to the style and purpose of the text. (Year 2 Strand 9)

What's on the CD-ROM

Same but more
- Click on pairs of cards to match sentences that say the same things in different ways.

What to do

In this lesson, children compare two versions of a sentence to see how using detail improves writing.

- Begin the activity by explaining that sentences vary in how much detail they present to the reader. Use some items to reinforce how a simple phrase can have detail added to it, for example, there is a difference between 'a dog' and 'a brown, plastic dog'. Discuss with the children the language choice and which wording gives more detail. Ask: *Why is this better? Why should we be adventurous in our writing?*

- Open 'Same but more' from the CD-ROM and click on two cards at a time. Read the sentences and ask the children if they can find two that go together.

- Hand out photocopiable page 33 'Same but more'. Ask the children to cut out the sentences and, as a first step, to put sentences about the same thing into pairs. Once they have done this, they can decide which sentence in each pairing gives the greater detail.

- When the children have completed the photocopiable sheet, let this lead on to a discussion about what has been added in the more detailed sentence.

Activity 10: Adjectives game

Objectives

To make adventurous word and language choices appropriate to the style and purpose of the text. (Year 2 Strand 9)
To use appropriate language to make sections hang together. (Year 2 Strand 10)

What's on the CD-ROM

Media resources
- Listen to 'Describing things' to hear descriptions of two common objects.

What to do

This activity can be used as a reminder to the children that description is a vital component of report writing.

- Open 'Describing things' from the CD-ROM and listen to the descriptions of two common objects. Can the children guess what the two objects are? (Post box and tree.) Explain to the children that they are going to play a speaking game that involves using good descriptions.

- Ask the children to sit in a circle. Explain how to play the 'Adjectives game': an object is passed around and the children take turns to think of a word that describes it, each child adding an adjective.

- For example, if the object is a jumper, the first child might begin with a 'red' jumper. The next child might add the word 'floppy', making the phrase 'a floppy, red jumper'. The next child might add the word 'old' – 'an old, floppy, red jumper'.

- Once they have exhausted the subject matter, move on to a different object to continue the game.

- Hand out photocopiable page 34 'Adjectives game'. Explain that this version of the activity gives a sentence starter, 'Here is a…', and some nouns the children can use for the subject. They have to decide which of the listed adjectives could fit – though trying some that do not can create tasty spiders and hairy teachers!

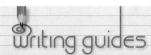

Object features

● List the features of chosen objects under each heading.

Movements

Colour

Shape

Smell

Noises it makes

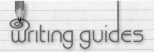

Pick it apart

- Think of something you could write about. Then try listing ten different things you could say about that subject.

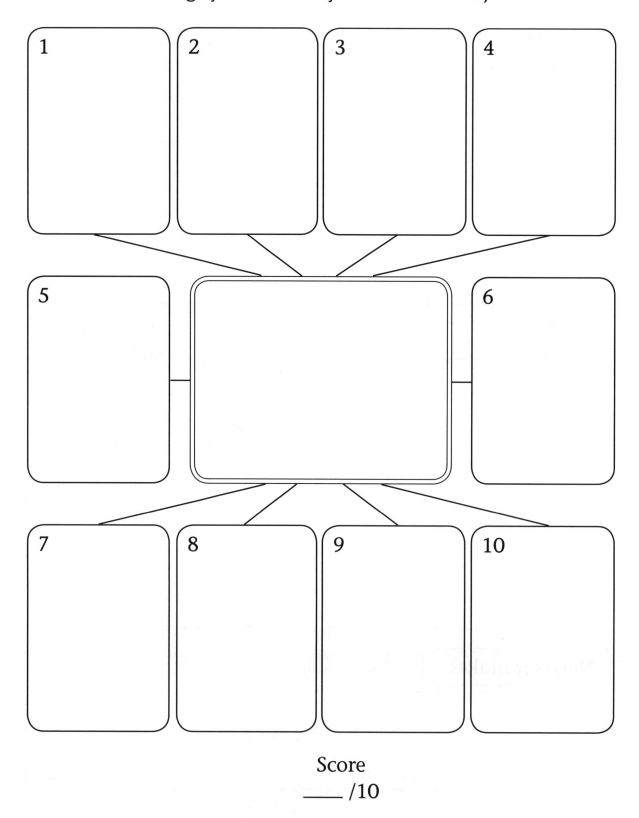

Score

____ /10

Superheroic reporting

● Draw a character in the centre of the page. Then list its features under the headings.

Looks like?

Gets from one place to another?

Special powers?

Always says the same catchphrase?

Changes?

Can be defeated by?

Tree splits

● Start with a subject. Think of three things you can say about it. Then say a bit more about each separate thing.

Illustrations © 2002, Garry Davies.

About me

- Write some facts about yourself on these cards.

My name	Colour of eyes	Height
Favourite activity	My age	Where I live
What I think about school	Favourite food	My best place to visit
Something I don't like	A person I like to be with	Favourite smell
Favourite colour	A picture of my face	When I grow up I want to be…

Is, are, has, have

● Try rebuilding these sentences.

Summer

playing with me.

has

is

We

got new trainers.

are

Joe

after spring.

My friends

have

good fun at school.

Illustrations © 2002, Garry Davies.

Subject cards

● Choose a card which will be the subject of your report writing. You will need to make some notes first.

what you can see through the classroom window	your friend	a shop you visit a lot
the weather today	the street where you live	your classroom
a packed lunch	your family	the school playground
your home	your teacher	a park where you play

About us

● Gather some notes about your group and write a report about your similarities and differences.

The colour of our eyes _____ _____ _____	**Our favourite activity** _____ _____ _____
Where we live _____ _____ _____	**What we think about school** _____ _____ _____
Our favourite foods _____ _____ _____	**Things we don't like** _____ _____ _____

Illustrations © 2010, Garry Davies.

Same but more

● Find sentences that are about the same thing. Can you see which sentence gives more detail?

If you push the switch, the light will flash.	The teddy has a button nose which I have sewn on.
The weather is sunny, but it is starting to rain.	The weather is sunny.
When the green person lights up, it is safe to cross the road.	The playground is warm.
The sun has made the playground warm.	The teddy has a button nose.
The light will flash.	It is safe to cross the road.

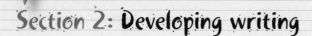
Adjectives game

● Match the adjectives to the sentence starter and endings to make new sentences.

Sentence starter

Here is a

Adjectives

creamy	creepy	dynamic	fast
hairy	happy	huge	kind
noisy	scary	sweet	tasty

Sentence endings

bus	teacher
cake	spider

Writing

Introduction

By this stage, the children will have explored some of the key features of constructing a report text, maintaining the four key aspects as shown on photocopiable page 18 'Reports' in Section 1:

● introduce a subject

● give some details

● use present tense

● organise information.

They will have involved themselves in thinking of details to present when reporting on a subject, moving from the general to the specific and using present-tense sentences.

Using the writing projects

In this section, the four key elements of report writing are developed through three different writing projects whose focus is: two creatures of your or the children's choice; a simulated location; and a planning activity that moves from questioning to planning a report text.

The children take the various skills and components that they developed in Section 2 and use them to produce complete texts. The three projects provide a range of opportunities to stimulate such writing – two of them being specifically linked to subjects while the third, a generic planner, can be applied to a range of subjects.

It is important to note that the two more guided tasks, 'Project 1: Creatures' and 'Project 3: Funland' also lend themselves to being applied to other subject matter, such as other animals or locations.

Using the CD-ROM resources

The interactive materials for each project are there to provide a way of gathering more subject matter that the children can shape into their report writing. The writing templates on the CD-ROM can be drawn upon as a way of organising and presenting writing, and also as a place to incorporate images – whether using those from the 'Image bank' or inviting the children to upload their own images – and so are extremely useful when children are working on subjects of their own choice, as well as on the reports used in this section.

Writing tips

● Give an introduction to your subject.
● Sort your text into sections that cover different things about your subject.
● Use the present tense.
● Write some facts and details.

Project 1: Creatures

Objectives

To convey information and ideas in simple non-narrative forms. (Year 1 Strand 9)
To create short simple texts on paper and screen that combine words with images. (Year 1 Strand 9)

What's on the CD-ROM

Creatures
- Answer the questions.

Media resources
- Use images as stimulus.

My report
- Compose a report.

What to do

This project begins with imaginary creatures and moves to the real thing – either in photos or in children's research.

- Open 'Creatures' from the CD-ROM. Invite the children to select a prompt question and ask them to make up a response to it for two imaginary creatures, making notes in the boxes. Then, using the images 'Snail' and 'Hippo' from the CD-ROM as a stimulus, ask the children to make up responses for these two real creatures.

- Having tried some examples, ask the children to describe their own real or imaginary creatures on photocopiable page 38 'Creatures'.

- Hand out photocopiable page 39 'Similar/different'. This provides a framework for the children to draw and compare the two creatures. Ask the children to note down similarities and differences between the creatures. They can refer back to their notes on photocopiable page 38 'Creatures'.

- Based on this stimulus, the children can now write a report about their two creatures. Ask the children to choose a writing template from the CD-ROM. Encourage them to structure their writing so that the two creatures take up separate paragraphs, creating an organised text.

Project 2: My report

Objectives

To write chronological and non-chronological texts using simple structures. (Year 1 Strand 10)
To draw on knowledge and experience of texts in deciding and planning what and how to write. (Year 2 Strand 9)

What's on the CD-ROM

Media resources
- Use 'Snail', 'Hippo' or 'Fun fair' as stimulus.

Report planner
- Plan a report.

My report
- Compose a report.

What to do

This general planning activity prompts children to unpick a subject in note form and reconstitute the notes in a written text.

- Open 'Describing things' from the CD-ROM. Listen to the people reporting on items and ask the children if they can guess what each speaker is talking about. (A post box and a tree.)

- Open 'Snail', 'Hippo' and 'Fun fair' from the CD-ROM. Ask the children to select one image and, using the question cards on photocopiable page 42 'My report', start to develop some thoughts and notes about the subject of their choice. The cards should be selected at random. If a question prompts a thought it has worked. If it does not, put it down and pick another.

- At this point, the children can either continue with the photo subject or choose another report subject. Open 'Report planner' from the CD-ROM and look at each section. Use these as the basis for either making notes or writing model sentences in shared writing.

- Hand out photocopiable page 43 'Report planner', which the children can now use as a planner for their own report text. The children can choose a template from the CD-ROM to create a written report.

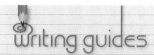

Project 3: Funland

Objectives

To write chronological and non-chronological texts using simple structures. (Year 1 Strand 10) To draw on knowledge and experience of texts in deciding and planning what and how to write. (Year 2 Strand 9)

What's on the CD-ROM

Media resources
- Use 'Fun fair' as stimulus.

Funland
- Roll your mouse over various attractions to see more information and highlight areas for focused writing.

My report
- Compose a leaflet using the writing template.

What to do

Using 'Funland' as a stimulus, the children produce a report on a location.

- Display the image of the fun fair from the CD-ROM. Ask the children to describe what they can see and for any experiences of similar fairs the children might have.

- Show them 'Funland' from the CD-ROM and ask the children to pick out different things they can see. Ask them to help you to make a list on the whiteboard of the features that are shown. Explain that in their report, it will be important that they do not leave anything out, as it will be used as an information guide for visitors.

- Start a separate list, making notes about the location. As you model the note-making, progress from a general statement about a subject to more specific details, such as how the go-karts move, how long each ride is, how much it costs and so on.

- Encourage the children to provide their own facts about the various features and the location on photocopiable pages 40 and 41 'Funland'. Roll your mouse over the examples on the CD-ROM activity, 'Funland', as a starter or stimulus, but ensure the children also devise their own ideas – such as a noise a ride makes or an extra animal in the Kiddie farm.

- Once they have done this, they should make some more detailed notes about the features on a separate piece of paper. Again, photocopiable page 14 '"Snails" notes' can be used to remind the children of the brief nature of note-making.

- Using the leaflet writing template, ask the children to create a guide to the park, incorporating images from the 'Image bank'. They can then use their notes to write a series of paragraphs about 'Funland'. For example, one paragraph could begin: 'The park is in the village. There is a big climbing frame and some swings. There are also tables for a picnic...'

- Print out the finished result and fold it to create the sort of guide leaflet that is handed out when you visit such attractions.

SCHOLASTIC
www.scholastic.co.uk

Creatures

Creature 2

What does it look like?

What does it eat?

Where does it live?

How does it feel?

Creature 1

How does it move?

What is it like?

What is it called?

What does it do?

Illustrations © 2002, Garry Davies.

Similar/different

| Creature 1 | Creature 2 |

Name _____

Picture

Name _____

Picture

Think of three similarities between these creatures.

1. _____

2. _____

3. _____

Think of three differences between these creatures.

1. _____

2. _____

3. _____

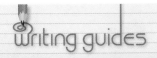

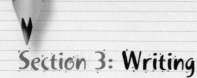

My report

● Cut out the cards, shuffle them and place them face downwards. Select a card at random and answer the question to make notes on your chosen report subject.

What is it?	What is it like?	What does it look like?
What does it feel like?	Does it make any noises?	What size is it?
What is good about it?	What is not good about it?	Where is it?
Why is it interesting?	Why would someone have something to do with it?	What is it for?

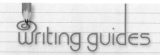

Report planner

● Plan a report text on your chosen subject.

This is a report about:

_____

Key words about this subject:

_____

_____

Important questions to think about:

_____

_____

_____

Important details to include:

_____

_____

_____

What will each paragraph be about?

_____

_____

_____

Illustrations © 2010, Garry Davies.

Review

Section 4 gives the children the opportunity to evaluate their own writing of specific reports, and reports in general, with the aim of encouraging them to develop some ideas for future texts. These activities can also provide a starting point for you to review the children's grasp of the features of writing highlighted throughout the book.

Self review

Photocopiable page 45 'Can you find…?' allows the children to draw on the skills they have learned in Sections 1 and 2. Using a text they have written, ask the children to find the features given on the photocopiable sheet and record examples. Looking at another piece of their report writing, can the children see similarities in different texts they have produced?

Peer review

To complete photocopiable page 46 'Questions answered', the children should look back at report texts they have created and find specific information that was presented in them. Ask the children to think of three questions that would be answered by the facts they have given. Invite the children to swap their questions and the report text they refer to with a partner. Ask them to discuss how clearly information is presented in each other's reports. Can they answer each other's questions? The children should then think about what they might tackle in a future report.

Teacher review

In assessing children's report writing at Key Stage 1, there are a number of checks that can be applied to their writing.

- Subject matter: check the degree to which children have engaged with the subject matter – both as a way of assessing their work and the subjects chosen. Look for lively writing that shows they were stimulated by the subject. They should also be displaying some degree of independent choice.

- Information gathering: their writing should demonstrate a degree of basic research, as children ask and answer questions about a subject.

- Organisation: at this stage, the children should be showing some first attempts at structuring their writing into an organised form. This will build into paragraphing and, more importantly, the capacity to organise longer stretches of text. Check the degree to which children have covered the range of subject matter available to their report and maintained consistency throughout their writing.

- Details: the children should be prompted to craft their writing to make it detailed and interesting, getting to some good factual statements.

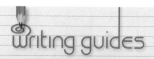

Can you find...?

- Look at a report text you have written.
- Find these things and write them here.

An opening sentence:

_____

_____

A sentence that gives a detail:

_____

_____

A sentence that uses present-tense verbs:

_____

_____

A sentence that tells us more about something:

_____

_____

Two sentences that are similar:

_____ | _____

_____ | _____

_____ | _____

Photocopiable **SCHOLASTIC** www.scholastic.co.uk

Questions answered

I wrote a report on

It answered these questions:

I could write a report on

and answer these questions:

Illustrations © 2002, Garry Davies.

writing guides

Teacher review

Child's name: _____   Date: _____

	AF5 Vary sentences for clarity, purpose and effect.	AF3 Organise and present whole texts effectively, sequencing and structuring information, ideas and events.	AF4 Construct paragraphs and use cohesion within and between paragraphs.	AF1 Write imaginative, interesting and thoughtful texts.	AF2 Produce texts which are appropriate to task, reader and purpose.	AF7 Select appropriate and effective vocabulary.
LEVEL 2	Mainly simple sentences. Consistent use of present tense.	Opening of report signalled by introducing the subject. Basic organisation of content.	Subject matter grouped into sections with some linking by simple pronouns.	Ideas are relevant to the subject of the report. Some interesting and descriptive word choices.	Some basic purpose established – text clearly devised to inform about a particular subject.	Some adventurous and descriptive words.
LEVEL 1	Simple sentences about subject matter. Some sentence-like structures, stating facts about the report subject.	Formulaic language used for example: 'It is...', 'It has got...'.	Simple connections between ideas for example 'and...'.	Basic information and ideas conveyed through appropriate word choice for example, related to the report subject. Some descriptive language, for example, colour, size, simple emotion.	Indicates the main purpose of the report with reference to the subject matter.	Mostly simple vocabulary.

Writing Assessment Focuses for Report texts (to be used in conjunction with Writing Guide: Reports) – refer to Primary Framework for literacy for a full set of Assessment Focuses for Key Stage 1.

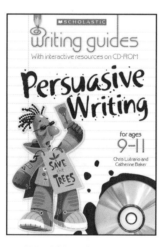

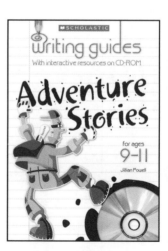